MW01641051

My son, Nathan, has been so kind helping me as my creative helper.
Thank you for sharing the kindness in your heart.

Stay in touch at www.piccopuppy.com and @PiccoPuppy on Instagram and Facebook.

Picco Puppy books are available in personalized, bilingual, French, Spanish, Italian, German, Chinese, and Japanese editions. Visit www.piccopuppy.com for more information.

A special thanks to my wonderful team: Zina Iugai (illustrator) and Brooke Vitale (editor).

Font Credits
Lost Brush by Stripes Studio
Marck Script by Denis Masharov
Cormorant Upright by Christian Thalmann
Century Schoolbook by Morris Fuller Benton
Copse by Dan Rhatigan
Josefin Sans by Santiago Orozco

First published in 2023 by Picco Puppy

Marketing Munch Pty Limited DBA Picco Puppy, PO Box 101, Roseville, NSW 2069, Australia
Picco Puppy® is a registered trademark of Marketing Munch Pty Limited

ISBN 978-1-76158-056-7

Share The Kindness In Your Heart

MICHAEL WONG • ZINA IUGAI

If there is one thing you can be,
then always, please be kind.
For in a world that's sometimes mean,
you'll stand out, you will find.

Kindness can be many things;
so where do we begin?
I'll share with you what kindness is,
come on now, let's jump in.

Kindness means you show your love
in all the things you do.
It's using manners—saying, "Please,"
"Excuse me," and "Thank you."

Kindness means you help your parents
with a household chore.
They'll appreciate your help,
and how their hearts will soar!

Kindness means you check on friends
and ask if they're okay.
Thoughtful gestures like that always
make another's day.

Kindness means you raise your hand
to help a classmate out.
This simple gesture warms the heart,
of that I have no doubt.

Kindness means you pick up trash
and help to clean the Earth.
It's a tiny selfless act
where you can show your worth.

Kindness means you donate clothes
that you no longer wear.
It's giving back to those in need
that shows you really care.

Kindness means you offer thanks
to brighten someone's day.
It's a gift that we can all
afford to give away.

But kindness isn't just for others,
be kind to your heart.
Yes, others will be kind to you,
but you must play your part.

I Wish You
Happiness

So, now you know what kindness is;
it is the greatest gift.
Passing on your kindness gives
another heart a lift.

Be kind to everyone you meet—
a smile can be the start.
So please remember, always ...

share the kindness in your heart!

Can You Spot the Famous People?

No matter what obstacles you face, believe in yourself and all that you are—
just like these famous people did. Can you spot all five in the book?

Can you spot a young Gail Halvorsen?

In 1948, while visiting Germany, pilot Gail Halvorsen was shocked to see how little the children had. So, he kindly dropped boxes of candy with handkerchief parachutes from his plane. For his act of kindness, Halvorsen became famous as "The Candy Bomber."

Can you spot a young Jacqueline Kiplimo?

During the 2010 Zheng-Kai Marathon, Jacqueline Kiplimo saw a disabled athlete struggling to drink water. She kindly ran alongside him for most of the race helping him at the water stations. This act of kindness cost her first place and a big prize.

Can you spot a young Jonas Salk?

Jonas Salk was born in 1914. In 1955, he developed the Polio vaccine. In order to help as many people as possible, Dr. Salk chose not to patent the Polio vaccine or profit from it. This act of kindness prevented millions of cases of paralysis and saved countless lives worldwide.

Can you spot a young Thomas Barnardo?

Thomas Barnardo was born in 1845. He set up homes to rescue children orphaned by a cholera outbreak. By the time of his death in 1905, his act of kindness had given 60,000 children a chance of a better life. Today, Barnardo's is the UK's largest children's charity.

Can you spot a young Yasuteru Yamada?

In 2011, there was a nuclear disaster in Fukushima, Japan. Yasuteru Yamada, a retired engineer, assembled a group of 400 elderly engineers. They kindly offered to replace younger engineers to protect them from the long-term health risks of radiation exposure.

Can You Spot the Dogs?

There are twelve cute dogs in the book. Can you spot them all?

Akita

Alaskan Malamute

Basset Hound

Boston Terrier

Brittany

English Springer Spaniel

Great Pyrenees

Havanese

Miniature Pinscher

Rhodesian Ridgeback

Rough Collie

Weimaraner

Hi, it's Michael here. Did you know there are more books in "The Unconditional Love Series"? I hope you collect them all.

Win a hardcover every month and claim your gift at www.piccopuppy.com/gift.

Michael Wong is an award-winning children's author. He is passionate about creating beautiful, empowering, diverse, and inclusive books for children. Michael lives with his wife and two children in Sydney, Australia.

Zina Jugai is an artist who fills her illustrations with light and atmosphere. She dreams of creating magical worlds with her illustrations.

The Unconditional Love Series

Available at Amazon, PiccoPuppy.com,
and all good bookstores.

Made in the USA
Middletown, DE
13 February 2024